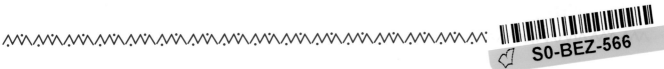

"Pay Attention, Please!"

Games and Activities to Improve Attention, Focus, and Listening Skills

by
Sherrill B. Flora

illustrated by
Chris Olson

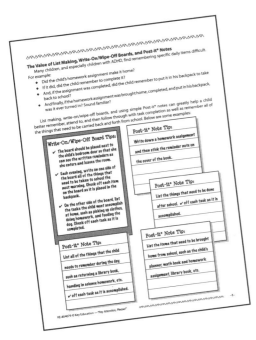

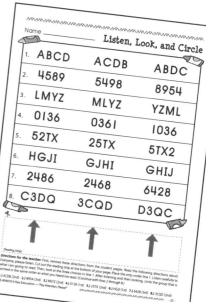

Publisher
Key Education—An imprint of Carson-Dellosa Publishing LLC
Greensboro, North Carolina

www.keyeducationpublishing.com

CONGRATULATIONS ON YOUR PURCHASE OF A KEY EDUCATION PRODUCT!

The editors at Key Education are former teachers who bring experience, enthusiasm, and quality to each and every product. Thousands of teachers have looked to the staff at Key Education for new and innovative resources to make their work more enjoyable and rewarding. Key Education is committed to developing and publishing educational materials that will assist teachers in building a strong and developmentally appropriate curriculum for young children.

PLAN FOR GREAT TEACHING EXPERIENCES WHEN YOU USE EDUCATIONAL MATERIALS FROM KEY EDUCATION PUBLISHING COMPANY, LLC

Credits
Author: Sherrill B. Flora
Creative Director: Annette Hollister-Papp
Cover Design: Annette Hollister-Papp
Illustrator: Chris Olson
Editors: Karen Seberg and Claude Chalk
Production: Key Education Staff

Resources and References

U.S. DEPARTMENT OF HEALTH AND HUMAN SERVICES
National Institutes of Health
NIH Publication No. TR-08-3572 (Revised 2008)
http://www.nimh.nih.gov/healthy/publications/attention-deficit-hyperactivity-disorder-easy-to-read-index.shtml

Special Note: Before completing any balloon activity, ask families about latex allergies. Also, remember that uninflated or popped balloons may present a choking hazard.

Key Education welcomes manuscripts and product ideas from teachers.
For a copy of our submission guidelines, please send a self-addressed, stamped envelope to:

Key Education Publishing Company, LLC
Acquisitions Department
Carson-Dellosa Publishing
PO Box 35665
Greensboro, NC 27425-5665

Standard Book Number: 978-1-602680-72-2
"Pay Attention, Please!"
Key Education—An imprint of Carson-Dellosa Publishing LLC
Copyright © 2010 by Carson-Dellosa Publishing LLC
PO Box 35665
Greensboro, North Carolina 27425-5665

01-135118091

Contents

Introduction

According to the National Institute of Mental Health (2008), children mature at different rates and have different personalities, temperaments, and energy levels. Most children get distracted, act impulsively, and struggle to concentrate at one time or another. It is normal for all children at times to be inattentive, hyperactive, and impulsive.

However, for children with ADHD, these behaviors are more severe and occur more often. To be diagnosed with the disorder, a child must have symptoms for six or more months and to a degree that is greater than other children of the same age.

Children who have symptoms of inattention may:

◆ Be easily distracted, miss details, forget things, and frequently switch from one activity to another

◆ Have difficulty focusing on one thing

◆ Become bored with a task after only a few minutes, unless they are doing something enjoyable

◆ Have difficulty focusing attention on organizing and completing a task or learning something new

◆ Have trouble finishing or turning in homework, often losing things (for example, pencils, supplies, or assignments) needed to complete tasks or activities

◆ Not seem to listen when spoken to

◆ Daydream, become easily confused, and move slowly

◆ Have difficulty processing information as quickly and accurately as others

◆ Struggle to follow instructions

Children who have symptoms of hyperactivity may:

◆ Fidget and squirm in their seats

◆ Talk nonstop

◆ Dash around, touching or playing with anything and everything in sight

◆ Have trouble sitting still during dinner, school, and story time

◆ Be constantly in motion

◆ Have difficulty doing quiet tasks or activities

Children who have symptoms of impulsivity may:

◆ Be very impatient

◆ Blurt out inappropriate comments, show their emotions without restraint, and act without regard for consequences

◆ Have difficulty waiting for things they want or waiting their turns in games

◆ Often interrupt conversations or others' activities

"Pay Attention, Please!" is a book filled with games and activities that help children with ADHD—and children who are otherwise wiggly and overly busy—learn how to pay better attention, increase their abilities to focus for longer periods of time, and improve listening skills. Children who are able to pay attention, focus their concentration, and become effective listeners are children who have a far greater chance of succeeding in school.

 KE-804079 © Key Education —*"Pay Attention, Please!"*

Schedules and Routines

Children with ADHD have trouble paying attention. They struggle to complete assignments, and other things going on in the classroom frequently distract them. Some children also have trouble controlling behaviors that negatively affect their relationships with both the other children and the teachers in the classroom. Children with ADHD benefit from routines; minimizing distractions and clearly outlining expectations help them to concentrate on the tasks at hand.

Posting a written schedule helps children know exactly what to expect through the day. Children with ADHD can become anxious when they are not sure what is going to happen next. Talk frequently about what event is happening or is about to happen.

Schedules and Routines at Home

Children with ADHD, because of their internal disorganization, function best when they live in homes that are orderly and organized, have consistent routines, and provide them with clear expectations. Parents, with the help of their children, are responsible for creating schedules and establishing the routines that best meet the needs of their individual families. Schedules for getting ready in the morning, following through with daily chores, and completing homework in the evening are only some of the areas where a written agenda can help greatly in developing a child's organizational skills.

Written Schedules

Schedules should be written, with space provided for children to check off each task as it is completed. Create a chart with pictures if the child isn't yet able to read. A daily or weekly schedule can be posted on the child's bedroom wall, a bulletin board, or the refrigerator.

Sit down with your child and fill out the schedule's activities together. Talk about what is planned for that day and anything special that may be happening later in the week. Always include the everyday expected activities on the chart, such as mealtimes and brushing teeth, as well as regularly scheduled events, such as dance lessons or athletic team practices. Also, include those activities that may not occur regularly, such as grocery shopping, a visit to the library, or a play date with a friend.

Reproducible Schedules: Reproducible daily and weekly schedules are found on pages 9 and 10. To save time and paper, copy the schedules on card stock, laminate them, and let children label them with washable markers. Encourage children to check off each task when it is completed. You may also copy the Cutout Symbols (page 11) on card stock and color and laminate them for use with the daily schedule. Children can attach the pieces with Velcro® to show the day's activities.

Structured Study Space

Many children with ADHD concentrate better in highly structured situations. Experts advise parents to provide their children with a quiet, uncluttered place to do homework or school projects. Parents should take a look at the space and ask themselves the following questions:

- ◆ Is this a quiet area where your child can study and work undisturbed?
- ◆ Is it conducive to developing good study habits?
- ◆ Do you have a comfortable chair for your child to sit on while studying?
- ◆ Is there adequate lighting where he reads?
- ◆ Are the needed supplies available for your child to complete schoolwork? (These may include paper, pencils, a pencil sharpener, erasers, a ruler, tape, a scissors, and a dictionary.)
- ◆ Are there special study materials as needed, such as index cards for creating flash cards?
- ◆ Is there a way for your child to organize the supplies, such as desk drawers or work bins?
- ◆ Do you have the books your child needs to complete assignments?

The Value of List Making, Write-On/Wipe-Off Boards, and Post-it® Notes

Many children, and especially children with ADHD, find remembering specific daily items difficult. For example:

- ◆ Did the child's homework assignment make it home?
- ◆ If it did, did the child remember to complete it?
- ◆ And, if the assignment was completed, did the child remember to put it in his backpack to take back to school?
- ◆ And finally, if the homework assignment was brought home, completed, and put in his backpack, was it ever turned in? Sound familiar?

List making, write-on/wipe-off boards, and using simple Post-it® notes can greatly help a child better remember, attend to, and then follow through with task completion as well as remember all of the things that need to be carried back and forth from school. Below are some examples:

Write-On/Wipe-Off Board Tips:

- ✔ The board should be placed next to the child's bedroom door so that she can see the written reminders as she enters and leaves the room.

- ✔ Each evening, write on one side of the board all of the things that need to be taken to school the next morning. Check off each item on the board as it is placed in the backpack.

- ✔ On the other side of the board, list the tasks the child must accomplish at home, such as picking up clothes, doing homework, and feeding the dog. Check off each task as it is completed.

Post-it® Note Tip:

Write down a homework assignment and then stick the reminder note on the cover of the book.

Post-it® Note Tip:

List the things that need to be done after school. ✔ off each task as it is accomplished.

Post-it® Note Tip:

List all of the things that the child needs to remember during the day, such as returning a library book, handing in science homework, etc.

✔ off each task as it is accomplished.

Post-it® Note Tip:

List the items that need to be brought home from school, such as the child's planner, math book and homework assignment, library book, etc.

Schedules and Routines at School

Adjustments and Modifications for Schedules and Work Space

◆ **Plan shorter assignments and work periods.** Providing shorter assignments and reducing work periods can give children a sense of completion and success. As children become more confident learners, the length of both assignments and work periods can be extended.

◆ **Give students breaks or free time between work periods.** Breaks should be about five minutes and take place away from the work area.

◆ **Cut or fold papers in half.** Students can be overwhelmed by assignments that appear to be long or overly crowded. Many children even appreciate papers that are folded into fourths. It is rewarding for students to feel as if they have completed one task before moving on to the next.

◆ **Alternate various activities.** Vary the types of activities and lessons presented in the classroom. For example, plan an activity that involves movement and active participation and then follow that lesson with a quiet activity. This type of variety helps children to maintain interest.

◆ **Use cueing strategies.** Try this technique to help students learn to identify when they are off task.

◆ **Separate distracting students.** Place struggling students apart from other students who may be distracting to them. Sit children by others who can be helpful and where positive relationships can be established.

◆ **Provide students with opportunities to move around the room.** Assigning classroom tasks, like passing out papers and making deliveries to the office, can help reduce frustration and boredom for children with ADHD.

◆ **Create classroom work contracts.** Work contracts can be effective tools for helping children improve task completion and better understand expectations. (See sample classroom work contracts on page 12.)

Teaching Organizational Skills

◆ **Employ daily assignment books.** A daily assignment book, even for nonreaders, is an excellent tool to help children become more organized as well as to keep parents informed. Parents can be asked to initial the book daily to confirm that their child brought information home and that they discussed schoolwork with their child. The routine of a daily assignment book can teach children to be responsible for carrying home information and help them remember to complete tasks.

◆ **Keep desks clear and clean.** Help children learn to keep their desks free of unnecessary materials. A cluttered desk creates undue confusion and disorganization for a child who already has difficulty organizing materials.

◆ **Provide different colors of notebooks.** Using a distinct color for each subject will help children to organize class notes.

◆ **Distribute My Weekly Assignment Planner.** Reproduce the planner on page 13 and use it to track assignments, tests, and due dates. This tool will help children organize and remember all of the tasks they need to accomplish during a week. For example, they can write down their assignments and other things they must bring to school or take home in order to complete the work. When a task is completed, children can place a check mark in the triangular box.

◆ **Apply a positive reinforcement program.** Use this strategy to emphasize the amount of time spent on tasks and to encourage the completion of work within the time given.

◆ **Use lists and Post-it® notes.** Lists help children remember things and keep tasks organized. The My To Do List on page 13 is a handy tool for organizing those pieces of information, especially for children who can only handle short reminders for specific tasks.

Ideas to Get Homework Assignments Home!

Children with ADHD often arrive home at the end of the day and are not sure what their homework assignments are. This creates confusion for the child and is frustrating for parents. No one is quite sure what the evening's homework entails. Following are some ideas that will make the process of completing homework easier for everyone:

- ◆ **Have a special space on the board for homework assignments.** Always write homework assignments in the same place on the board and in large print. Then, the child with ADHD will know that he is copying the correct information.

- ◆ **Leave homework assignments on the board all day.** Write assignments on the board first thing in the morning and leave them up all day long. This ensures that the child has had enough time to copy down the assignments.

- ◆ **Use homework journals.** Every student should have a homework journal in which to write down assignments. You may make copies of My Weekly Assignment Planner (page 13) and staple the pages into a booklet. Before dismissal, quickly check everyone's journal to make sure that the assignments were copied correctly.

- ◆ **Strategically place the student's desk.** Position the ADHD child's desk close to the board so that the child can easily see what is written on it.

- ◆ **Provide homework handouts.** Homework handouts will benefit those students who are overly challenged by copying from the board. You may use the assignment planner (page 13) by simply filling in the class's assignments, copying them, and distributing them to the children.

- ◆ **Utilize the school's Web site.** If your school has a Web site where homework assignments can be posted daily, make sure that all students and their families are aware of this resource.

Clocks

Clocks are wonderful for simply learning how to identify numbers and to begin the concept of telling time. Choose a number of activities that happen at the same time each day, such as arrival at school, lunch, snack, naps, going home, etc. Then, make paper plate clocks and set the hands to display those times. When it is time for each activity, show children that the time on the real clock matches the paper plate clock. Let children make their own paper plate clocks to take home. They can set their clocks for bedtime or getting-up-in-the-morning time.

Study Carrels

Would the use of a study carrel, work cubby, or any area where work can be done alone aid the child's progress? To insure a private space in which the child may work, help her create a study carrel.

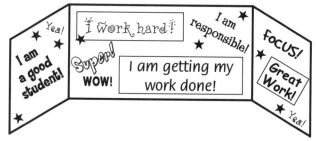

What you need: three-section display board, paper, scissors, glue stick, markers

What you do: Invite the child to draw pictures and write encouraging messages to post inside her carrel. Allow plenty of time for her to decorate it any way she wants. Make sure she is allowed to use the carrel in class or at home whenever she needs to block out distracting visual stimuli.

Daily Schedule

Today is: _____ Date: _____

Time	Activity

Time	Activity

Weekly Schedule

(Directions can be found on page 5.)

Sunday	Monday	Tuesday	Wednesday	Thursday	Friday	Saturday
↓	↓	↓	↓	↓	↓	↓

KE-804079 © Key Education —*"Pay Attention, Please!"*

(Directions can be found on page 5.)

Cutout Symbols for the Daily Schedule

get dressed	brush teeth	eat breakfast	eat lunch

eat dinner	comb hair	go to dance lesson	go to sports practice

grocery shop	go to medical appointment	get on school bus	eat afternoon snack
	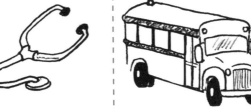		

do homework	do daily chores	feed the pet	put homework in backpack

pick up toys	get ready for bed	read bedtime story	
		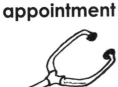	

(blank—make your own)

(Directions can be found on page 7.)

Sample Classroom Work Contracts

Contracts can be effective tools for managing behavior, improving task completion, and for motivating positive school performance. When a contract is written, be sure to include a clear definition of what is expected of the child, the positive consequence for achieving the expectation, the negative consequence if the expectation is not met, what the student and adult involved are expected to do, and a plan for achieving the desired objectives. Following are two examples of contracts that are effective with younger children:

Weekly Contract for: _____

Goal: _____

| Monday | Tuesday | Wednesday | Thursday | Friday |

Reward: _____ Date: _____

Signed: _____ Signed: _____
(Student's name) *(Teacher's name)*

✂ -

Contract for: _____	M	T	W	Th	F
Goal 1:					
Goal 2:					
Goal 3:					
Goal 4:					
Goal 5:					

Reward: _____ Date: _____

Signed: _____ Signed: _____
(Student's name) *(Teacher's name)*

 KE-804079 © Key Education — *"Pay Attention, Please!"*

My To Do List

My Weekly Assignment Planner

Monday

Tuesday

Wednesday

Thursday

Friday

(Directions can be found on page 7.)

(Directions can be found on pages 7 and 8.)

Busy Kids—Creative Kids!
The Creative Strengths of Children with ADHD

Although ADHD may make learning difficult, it can also provide a person with unique ways of seeing things that most other people cannot see. Many famous artists have struggled with learning. Leonardo da Vinci sometimes wrote backward; his writing provides evidence of possible perceptual problems.

Children with ADHD often have above average IQs and are usually highly creative, artistic, intuitive, inventive, and humorous. Many display other positive characteristics that make them special individuals. Helping children celebrate the positive and creative traits of ADHD will give them the pride and courage needed to face each day and help them grow up to be happy, productive adults.

Finding Hidden Talents, Interests, and Hobbies

Children should be encouraged to seek out hidden talents and explore a variety of interests. By discovering their own special talents, developing new interests, or becoming involved with hobbies, children are kept meaningfully occupied and are continually learning. Here are a few examples of things that could interest an active child in your life: playing a musical instrument, drawing cartoons, painting, beading and jewelry making, taking responsibility for the family pet, learning about dinosaurs, or beginning a collection (for example, stamps, coins, small cars, action figures, or books).

Preparing for Projects

Busy Boxes

Busy boxes are easily assembled and can provide hours of great fun for an active child. Fill each busy box with supplies that relate to a particular type of activity. Assemble the boxes with themes that will maintain the child's interest. Keep adding to the boxes so that some new interest is created each time the child chooses one to play with. Here are four examples of easy-to-make busy boxes:

Office Busy Box: Instead of using a box, store the materials for the office busy box in an old briefcase. Fill the briefcase with a ruler, a stapler, a paper punch, stickers, pencils, pens, paper, envelopes, and postcards (to encourage letter and postcard writing), Post-it® notes, a date book, a calculator, an old phone, and a tape recorder.

Stamping/Scrapbooking Busy Box: Fill a box with rubber stamps, ink pads, scissors, stickers, colorful construction paper, card stock, markers, photos, a glue stick, double-stick tape, and a scrapbook.

Junk Art Box: Use an old sewing basket and supply it with buttons, fabric, needle, thread, sequins, watercolor paper, watercolors, paintbrushes, scissors, a glue stick, construction paper, scraps of wallpaper, ribbons, crayons, colorful pencils, coloring books, old magazines with pictures for collages, and anything else you think would be fun to have in the huge art basket!

Play Dough Busy Box: Fill a box with containers of colorful play dough or clay, a rolling pin, waxed paper, cookie cutters, and plastic utensils. Here is a recipe for The Best Basic Play Dough:

What you need: 3 cups (0.71 L) flour, 1½ cups (0.35 L) salt, 3 tablespoons (44.36 mL) cream of tartar, 3 cups (0.71 L) water, 3 tablespoons (44.36 mL) vegetable oil, food coloring

What you do: Add the food coloring to the water. Mix the flour, salt, cream of tartar, vegetable oil, and colored water together in a saucepan. Cook over a low heat, stirring constantly, until the dough is no longer sticky. Cool the dough and place it into a plastic bag that seals tightly. Knead the dough in the plastic bag for several minutes and then store the dough in the refrigerator in airtight containers.

Anytime Art Activities

Monster Bubbles

What you need: metal coat hanger, bottle of bubble solution (or use the recipe below), pizza pan

What you do: Pour the bubble solution into the pizza pan. Bend the coat hanger into a circle to make a monster bubble wand using the hook as a handle. Dip the bubble wand into the bubble solution and wave it slowly to create some enormous bubbles.

> **Bubble Recipe:** 1 gallon (3.78 L) cold water
> 1 cup (0.24 L) liquid detergent (Allow this to sit overnight in a cool place.)
> 2 tablespoons (29.57 mL) liquid glycerin (available at most pharmacies)

Additional Wand Ideas: Use the plastic rings from a six-pack of soda pop, rings from canning jars, or plastic rings cut from various sizes of plastic lids (margarine lids, coffee can lids, etc.). Let the children experiment with blowing bubbles from different sizes of rings.

Magic Clay

What you need: 2⅔ cups (0.63 L) water, 1 cup (0.24 L) cornstarch dissolved in ½ cup (118 mL) cold water

What you do: Heat the water over low heat until bubbly. Remove it from the heat and add the dissolved cornstarch solution. Stir it quickly, mixing with your hands if necessary as it cools. Add a bit more water if needed. If allowed to dry at room temperature for 36 hours, it will harden and can be painted.

Stringing Beads

Bead stringing is an ancient and colorful art and is excellent for developing fine-motor skills. There are many good manufactured kits of beads and strings for use in the classroom. Unfortunately, children are never able to take home their finished creations when they use a manufactured kit. Provide macaroni and cut pieces of straws for children to string. They can practice the fine-motor skill of stringing beads and will be able to share their creations with their families.

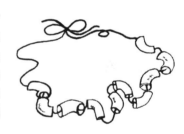

Rubbery Goop

What you need: 2 cups (0.47 L) baking soda, 1½ cups (0.35 L) water, 1 cup (0.24 L) cornstarch

What you do: Place all of the ingredients in a saucepan over medium heat and stir until smooth. Boil the mixture while stirring constantly until it is thick. Remove it from the heat and let it cool. Now, invite children to enjoy the feel and texture, as well as the movement, of this rubbery goop!

Slimy Goop

What you need: ½ cup (118 mL) white glue, food coloring (optional), ¼ cup (59 mL) liquid starch, wooden spoon

What you do: Place all of the ingredients in a bowl and mix them thoroughly with a wooden spoon, craft stick, or tongue depressor. Let the children get their fingers sticky and have a lot of "goopy" fun!

Cereal Mosaics

At the grocery store, there are many dry cereals that are bright with artificial coloring. Give each child a piece of construction paper or poster board with the outline of a flower on it. Fill the insides of the flowers with glue. Have children place colorful cereal pieces inside their flowers.

Listening and Attending Skills

Listening and Its Importance

Learning to listen and pay attention are essential skills for everyday living. Children with ADHD often experience extreme difficulties with these important skills. Some children are not able to screen out what is unimportant from the many sounds they hear, and so they listen to everything. They may also not be very skilled at sustaining attention and therefore miss large chunks of information.

Listening and an increased ability to pay attention are skills that need to be taught, especially to children with ADHD who have difficulties focusing on information or directions they are given. It is virtually impossible to "pay attention" when you are not "listening"—the two skills go hand in hand.

To build a foundation of effective listening skills, children need to develop the following:

◆ **Sound discrimination**—distinguishing between sounds that are the same and sounds that are different.

◆ **Awareness and recognition of sounds**—developing an awareness and recognition of common sounds that are heard in various everyday situations (for example, traffic sounds, a telephone's ring, birds chirping, etc.).

◆ **Identification of sounds**—being able to identify and name everyday sounds. Children at this stage also begin to develop phonemic and letter-sound awareness.

◆ **Sound concepts**—identifying if sounds are high or low, loud or soft, near or far away, and so on.

Research has provided evidence that listening and attending skills can be greatly improved when these skills are practiced. The following games and activities will help children learn to pay better attention and to better understand what they have heard.

Science of Listening Activities

Experimenting with Sound

To help children learn how to become better listeners, it makes sense that children must first understand what they are being asked to learn and practice. They need to become familiar with sound as a concept. The following fun activities will let children discover more about sound, listening, and paying attention:

◆ **Feel where speech sounds come from.** Have children touch their own throats while making various sounds to feel the vibrations produced by their vocal cords.

◆ **Make some sounds.** Invite each child to make a musical comb by folding a piece of waxed paper around a pocket comb and then pressing it against his mouth and humming both loudly and softly.

◆ **Listen to the sounds of a beating heart.** Use a stethoscope to let children listen to one another's heartbeats.

 KE-804079 © Key Education —*"Pay Attention, Please!"*

Sound Travels

Place a ticking watch or clock on a board, tabletop, or any flat surface that will serve as a conductor. Have each child place an ear to the board to discover that sound is traveling through the wood as well as through the air.

Sound—Feel It, See It, Hear It!

Hammer two large nails or spikes to opposite ends of a piece of wood. (See illustration.) Stretch a heavy rubber band or piece of tire tubing between the nails. Invite children to pluck the rubber band. The vibrations will be felt through the board and nails, they will be seen as the rubber band moves, and they will be heard as plunking sounds. Try tightening the rubber band to get a higher pitch.

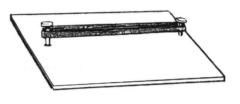

Listening and Identifying Common Sounds Activities

Everyday Sounds

Help children recognize well-known sounds like the ones they hear at home. For this activity, you will need a tape or CD with different commonly heard sounds such as a tap running, a toilet flushing, a vacuum cleaner's motor, etc. Children will enjoy guessing what sounds they are hearing.

Outside Sounds

Display a picture of a place such as a park, zoo, or airport. Then, ask children to think of the sounds they would hear if they were there. Make those sounds and record them. Play the tape on another day and let the children guess what they are hearing. (When using this activity in an ESL classroom, the next step would be to learn the proper vocabulary for the noises such as *footsteps*, a *car honking*, etc.)

Variation: Use the two reproducible pictures provided on page 22 to help children further explore outside sounds. Copy a picture for each child. Ask children to circle everything in the picture that they think is making a sound. Then, discuss—and make—the sounds when they have completed their papers.

Now Hear This!

What you need: a variety of items that can be used to make noise, such as paper to crumple, a plastic glass and spoon to tap, a piece of chalk to write on a blackboard, two blocks to clap, a closed container filled with pebbles, a bottle to blow into, etc. Put each of the items in a small paper bag.

What you do: Choose one child to close or cover her eyes. Invite another child to select one of the bags, and, at a signal, make a noise with the contents. If the first child can guess what made the noise, she may have the next turn to choose a bag.

Variation: Place small musical instruments in the bags, such as a handbell, shaker, maraca, etc., or simply use movements for the child to identify, such as clapping hands, snapping fingers, stamping feet, etc.

Matching Sounds

Fill small identical containers with rice, sand, small nails, salt, beans, cotton batting, etc. Make sure you have a pair of each. Have the children shake the containers and listen carefully to find each set of two that sound the same.

Be a Noisemaker

Every young child enjoys being a noisemaker, especially when playing with blocks, trucks, balls, or musical instruments. During group time, distribute two or three common objects and/or musical instruments to each child while the children sit on the floor in a circle. Allow the group a few minutes to discover what sounds they can make with their materials. Then, direct the children to arrange their noisemakers on the floor in a special way. (This helps the children to "turn off" the noisemakers.) Begin the activity by asking children to use their objects to make very soft sounds and then ask them to make sounds that are louder.

Talk about the materials they used to make the sounds and what they did to change the dynamics. Continue the activity by choosing a child to be a noisemaker. Direct the remaining children to cover their eyes and listen carefully for a sound that will be made by the chosen child. The noisemaker then selects one of the instruments, walks to another part of the classroom, and makes a soft sound behind a designated area. Have the children uncover their eyes. Ask: "Where is the noisemaker?" and "What did the noisemaker use to make the noise?" Repeat the activity with a new noisemaker.

Listening to Voices and Language Activities

Telephone

If possible, borrow two telephones or make do with toy phones and a teacher's creativity. Set up two "homes" or "offices" out of sight of each other (have children face away from each other or place one behind a screen). The children can introduce themselves over the phone and guess to whom they are talking. This activity will also provide a means of teaching proper phone etiquette.

Sounds through a Classroom Juice-Can Telephone

You will need two juice cans and a long piece of string. Make a hole in the bottom of each can. Thread one end of the string through each hole. Tie a knot or fasten the string around a toothpick inside of each can. Ask one child to hold a can and give the other one to a partner. Have the children walk away from each other so that the string is pulled taut. One child may talk into his can while his partner puts her ear to the open end of the other can and listens. Ask, "How did the sound travel?"

Listen Carefully

Tell the children to close their eyes and be very quiet. Then, silently walk around the children, tap one on the shoulder, and whisper a request in that child's ear, such as to recite a nursery rhyme, sing a song, or simply say "hello, friends." That child then performs the request. When the child is finished, invite the other children to open their eyes and guess who was talking.

Listen to This

Children are always fascinated with the voices they hear on a tape recorder, especially if the voices to which they are listening belong to them or to people they know. Make a tape of you telling stories or reciting finger plays. Provide a space where individual children can go off in a corner to replay their favorites. It is best if the recorder can be equipped with a headphone set. Then, let the children make tape recordings of themselves telling stories to listen to and enjoy.

 KE-804079 © Key Education —"Pay Attention, Please!"

Who's That Talking?

This is a fun activity that parents can do with their children at home. Turn a favorite television show into a listening game. Watch the show for a few moments together. Then, ask the child to close his eyes and listen carefully. After a character from the show speaks, ask the child who is speaking. Tell the child to open his eyes to discover if he was correct. Parents should also have the fun of taking a turn.

Games to Build Listening Skills

Play Traditional Simon Says

The old favorite, Simon Says, has been delighting children for generations. Even though it is a simple listening game, it is very effective. Let children take turns being "Simon" as the others listen carefully for each direction.

Whistle

Children really love this game. It is good for developing gross motor skills and for increasing listening skills. When you give the signal, children may walk in any direction. When you blow a whistle, they must stop immediately. Those who do not stop when they hear the whistle are asked to sit down. Continue with another movement such as run, crawl, skate, or tiptoe until only one child is left. This last player wins the game.

This is a good game to play with children at the beginning of the year. It will teach them that when they hear a whistle, they should stop and listen to you. This activity will certainly make rounding up everyone on the playground a lot easier!

Alert Game

Cut large squares, circles, triangles, and other shapes of various colors from construction paper. Have children begin in a straight line. On your command, they will walk rapidly, following each instruction they hear.

For example: Walk to a red triangle; touch something wood; walk to a blue circle; touch something metal; walk to an orange square; touch something made of cloth; walk to a black circle; touch something made of rubber, etc. Depending on the ages and abilities of your children, you can make the directions as easy or difficult as you wish.

Hot and Cold Game

The game of hot and cold is a traditional game that almost everyone has played. Choose a child to be "it." "It" covers her eyes while another child hides a small object in the classroom. As "it" begins to search for the object, the other children guide her by saying "hot" if she is near the object and "cold" if she is moving farther away from it. Once "it" finds the object, she is next to hide it and choose another child to search while listening for help from classmates.

Listening and Literacy Games and Activities

Talk, Talk, and Talk Some More!

Whenever and wherever you are—talk with your child. When you are shopping or working around the house or outside gardening, discuss what you are doing or tell stories about when you did these same daily activities as a child. Sometimes, we don't think that children are listening to us when they really are.

Classroom teachers can do the same thing. Share stories from your own childhood. Compare and contrast as you talk about things that are still the same and things that are now different.

Story Time Can Help Improve Listening and Attending Skills

Before the Story: Before reading a story to children, show them the book and discuss the cover. Point out the illustration on the front and talk about the author who wrote the book and the person who illustrated it. Tell students something interesting about the story to pique their interest. Providing children with some prior knowledge and getting them excited about the story will increase their listening and attending skills.

During the Story: As you read the story, ask questions and let children try to predict what will happen next. This ensures that children are listening in order to stay involved with the story. Continue to read and when you come to the answers for the questions you asked—or if the story just verified whether or not the children's predictions were correct—stop and review what the children had said or predicted about the story.

After the Story: When you have finished reading the story, discuss the ending with the children. Were their predictions accurate or was there a surprise ending? What clues were provided in the story that helped children come to their conclusions?

Providing children with "before the story," "during the story," and "after the story" questions and conversation will help them become active listeners thereby improving their abilities to pay attention and concentrate.

Read Favorite Books Over and Over

Teachers love hearing the words "please, read it again!" This means that children were engaged in listening to the story and understood what they heard. Children who want to hear the same stories over are learning how to direct their attention and become involved with the language of the story.

Play "Add-to-the Story"

Choose one child to begin a story, for example, "Once upon a time there was a little frog who lived on a very little lily pad." Then, ask a second child to add another sentence to the story, such as, "The poor frog was just too big for the lily pad, so he decided to move." A third child may add another sentence, and so on. Each child must listen carefully in order to keep the story moving forward and make sense. This is a wonderful game to enhance listening skills. Choosing children to contribute in random order—and more than once—helps ensure that they will continue to listen closely throughout the activity.

Picture Books

Choose a favorite picture book about farm animals. Find picture cards or plastic toy animals that correspond with the text and distribute them to the children. As you read the story aloud, when a particular farm animal is mentioned, the children holding the matching animal may generate the sounds that animal makes.

Alphabet Letter Games

Add a Word: Choose a child to say a word. The next child must say a word that begins with the final consonant sound of the previous word. (See illustration.) Continue until every child has had a chance to add a word.

Name Game: Begin with the letters in a child's name. Help the child come up with a word that begins with each letter in the name. For example: **Kent**—**k**ite, **e**lephant, **n**est, **t**ent.

dog, gum, mop, pin, not, ten, and so on . . .

Tongue Twisters and Alliteration

Choose a letter and then have children think of a sentence where almost every word begins with that same letter. For example: **T**—**T**odd **t**old **T**ed **t**o **t**ip his **t**op hat.

Here are several delightful tongue twisters:

Peter Piper picked a peck of pickled peppers.
Did Peter Piper pick a peck of pickled peppers?
If Peter Piper picked a peck of pickled peppers,
Where's the peck of pickled peppers
Peter Piper picked?

She sells seashells by the seashore.
The shells she sells are surely seashells.
So, if she sells shells by the seashore,
I'm sure she sells seashore shells.

How much wood would a woodchuck chuck
If a woodchuck could chuck wood?
He would chuck, he would,
as much as he could,
And chuck as much as a woodchuck would
If a woodchuck could chuck wood.

A skunk sat on a stump and thunk
  the stump stunk,
but the stump thunk the skunk stunk.

Silly Rhymes and Rhyming Books

Create silly rhymes with your students, the sillier the rhyme the better, such as "The bee up in the tree fell on his knee and screamed EEEEEEE!" This activity will help children listen for words that sound the same and identify rhyming patterns. Here are some stories to share that are written in rhyme:

Guarino, Deborah. *Is Your Mama a Llama?* Illustrated by Steven Kellogg. (Scholastic, 1989)
Hoberman, Mary Ann. *The Seven Silly Eaters*. Illustrated by Marla Frazee. (Harcourt, 1997)
Kirk, Daniel. *Skateboard Monsters*. Illustrated by the author. (Puffin, 1995)
Martin, Bill. *Chicka Chicka Boom Boom*. Illustrated by Lois Ehlert. (Beach Lane Books, 2009)
Seuss, Dr. *Green Eggs and Ham*. Illustrated by the author. (Random House, 1960)
Sierra, Judy. *Wild about Books*. Illustrated by Marc Brown. (Knopf, 2004)
Speed, Toby. *Brave Potatoes*. Illustrated by Barry Root. (Putnam, 2002)
Spinelli, Eileen. *The Best Time of Day*. Illustrated by Bryan Langdo. (Harcourt, 2005)

Listen and Follow Directions Reproducible Activities (Pages 23–25)

The three reproducible activities found on pages 23–25 will help increase listening skills and the ability to follow directions. Complete directions are found on each reproducible activity's page.

(Directions can be found on page 17.)

At the Zoo

Name _____

✂ --

At the Playground

Name _____

Name _____

Learn How to Listen

✂ -

Directions for the teacher: Each child will need a copy of this page; a pencil; and a pink, a blue, and a red crayon. Say to the children, "I would like you to listen very carefully and do exactly what I tell you to do to the picture of the rabbit. When we are finished with this page you will understand important ways to be a good listener." Then, read the following directions, leaving plenty of time for students to complete each task. **1.** Print your name on the line. **2.** We listen with our ears. Color the rabbit's ears pink. **3.** When we listen, we should look at the person who is talking. Draw blue circles around the rabbit's eyes to help us remember to look. **4.** We should stop what we are doing when someone talks. Color the stop sign red to help us remember to stop what we are doing and listen to what is being said. If we don't understand what the person is saying, we should ask the person to repeat it. **5.** Turn off distractions so that we can be better listeners. Choose a crayon and put an X on the radio and an X on the television to remind us to turn off extra noise. **6.** Now, look at your papers. Can you remember some of the "good listening" suggestions?

(listening skills)

Name _____ # Fun on the Farm

Directions for the teacher: The children will need a copy of this activity and crayons. Read the following directions aloud: **1.** Color the trees green. **2.** Color the duck in the pond yellow. **3.** Color the horse brown. **4.** Color the pig pink. **5.** Color the barn red. **6.** Draw a boy in front of the barn. **7.** Draw a cloud in the sky.

✂- -

(listening skills)

Name _____ # Schoolroom Fun!

ABCDEFGHIJKLMNOPQRSTUVWXYZ
123456789

Ms. Smith

cat

$\begin{array}{r} 3 \\ +\,4 \\ \hline \end{array}$

Directions for the teacher: The children will need a copy of this activity and crayons. Read the following directions aloud: **1.** Find the girl with two pigtails. Color her hair yellow. **2.** Find the boy with the curly hair. Color his shirt brown. **3.** Find the boy with the short hair. Color his hair red. **4.** Find the girl with the long ponytail. Color her shirt pink. **5.** Color the apple red. **6.** Color the pencil cup green. **7.** If you can, answer the math problem.

∧∧∧∧∧∧∧∧∧∧∧∧∧∧∧∧∧∧∧∧∧∧∧∧∧∧   KE-804079 © Key Education —"Pay Attention, Please!"

Listen, Look, and Circle

1.	ABCD	ACDB	ABDC
2.	4589	5498	8954
3.	LMYZ	MLYZ	YZML
4.	0136	0361	1036
5.	52TX	25TX	5TX2
6.	HGJI	GJHI	GHIJ
7.	2486	2468	6428
8.	C3DQ	3CQD	D3QC

(Reading Strip)

Directions for the teacher: First, remove these directions from the student pages. Then, read the following directions aloud: Everyone, please listen. Cut out the reading strip at the bottom of your page. Place the strip under line 1. Listen carefully to what I am going to read. Then, look at the three choices in line 1. After listening and then looking, circle the group that is printed in the same order as what you heard me read. *(Pause.)* In line 1, circle ACDB. *(Continue with lines 2 through 8.)*

1.) ACDB (2nd) **2.)** 8954 (3rd) **3.)** MLYZ (2nd) **4.)** 0136 (1st) **5.)** 25TX (2nd) **6.)** HGJI (1st) **7.)** 6428 (3rd) **8.)** 3CQD (2nd)

Focus and Concentration

Information about Focus and Concentration Skills

Many children have trouble learning how to focus and concentrate. These skills are especially difficult for children with ADHD. Today's advanced technologies have given this young generation so much stimulation that children often expect the world to move rapidly; they do not appreciate the fact that sometimes people must slow down in order to think hard about something. However, developing and improving concentration is not an impossible task. There are numerous activities that can improve these skills while also enhancing memory skills.

Some of the many activities that children enjoy and that will improve concentration include putting together puzzles, making models, learning how to dance or how to do karate, drawing and painting, and learning how to perform special chores around the house. There has also been research to support that playing certain computer and video games may actually build focus and concentration abilities in children with ADHD.

This is also a good place to note that the term *attention deficit hyperactivity disorder* is not always an accurate description of the disorder. Many children with ADHD actually experience periods of "**overfocusing**." People with ADHD have attention systems that are not properly regulated. So, although children with ADHD experience a deficit in attention skills, they can also experience over- or hyperfocusing. This is most likely to happen when children are playing a video game or watching TV. Unless an adult intervenes or something else happens to disrupt the child's intense concentration, hours can pass without the child even realizing it. During periods of hyperfocus, the child is not aware that he is concentrating so intensely or for such a long period of time.

Special Note: Always supervise the amount of time that children are allowed to watch television or play computer or video games.

Games of Skills and Strategies

Board Games

Board games improve concentration and are fun to play. Often, the best way to learn something new is to teach it through games. Checkers, Chutes and Ladders®, Candy Land®, memory match games, and Clue® (for older children) are excellent tools for teaching social skills, learning how to take turns, and developing thinking, strategy, and problem-solving skills. Keep games simple and make sure the directions are clear—often children with ADHD have low frustration levels and may not understand all of a game's rules. The purpose of playing games (besides having fun) is to help children pay attention to and evaluate what is happening with each move on the game board and to develop and use their own strategies as they play.

 KE-804079 © Key Education —"Pay Attention, Please!"

/\

Card Games

Card games are excellent for helping to increase a child's ability to concentrate. Here are the rules for some easy, traditional card games to play with a standard 52-card deck:

War

1. Shuffle the cards. Deal all of the cards to the players. Each player places his cards facedown in a pile.

2. Each player turns over her top card. The card with the highest value wins and that player collects all of the cards played that turn. The cards that are won are added to the bottom of the player's card pile. When two or more players turn over cards with the same value, a "war" begins.

3. For the war, those players each place three cards from their piles facedown on the table and turn their next cards faceup. Whoever has the card with the highest value wins all of the cards from the war. If there is a second tie, three more cards are added by the players involved in the war, and the process is repeated.

4. The game is over when one player has won all of the cards.

Crazy Eights

1. Shuffle and deal five cards to each player. Place the remaining cards facedown in the center of the table to create a draw pile. Turn over the top card to make a discard pile next to the draw pile.

2. The players look through their cards and arrange them by suits from the lowest to the highest number in each suit.

3. The first player may play any card that matches the number or suit of the card just played. For example, if a three of hearts is on top of the discard pile, a player may play any heart or any other three. Eights are wild and may be used by a player on any turn to change the suit to be played.

4. If a player cannot match the top card in the discard pile, he must keep drawing cards from the draw pile until he can play a card.

5. The first player to play all of her cards is the winner.

Rummy

1. Shuffle and deal five cards to each player. Place the remaining cards facedown in the center of the table to create a draw pile. Turn over the top card to make a discard pile next to the draw pile.

2. The goal is to collect sets of cards—two or three of a kind or two or three consecutive cards of the same suit.

3. Each turn consists of two parts. First, the player draws a card—either the top card from the draw pile or the top card from the discard pile. Second, the player must discard a card faceup on top of the discard pile.

4. The game is won when a player can lay down all of his cards in proper sets.

Go Fish

1. Shuffle the cards. Deal five cards to each player. Place the remaining cards facedown in the center of the table—this is the fishing pond!

2. The players look through their cards and arrange them according to the numbers on the cards.

3. The first player asks for a card from one of the other players, for example, "Do you have any fives?" If the player has the card asked for, he gives it to the first player. If not he says, "Go fish," and the first player draws a card from the pond.

4. The player keeps the turn as long as he keeps getting the cards he asked—or went fishing—for. When a player collects four cards with the same number, he lays them down in a set.

5. When a player is out of cards the game is over. The player with the most sets wins.

Observational Games and Activities

Focus and Count Reproducible Activity (Page 32)

Directions:

1. Have the child count the **cows** and time her while she does so. Record her answer and the amount of time it took.

2. Cover the puzzle with a sheet of paper. Time her as she slowly slides the paper down and counts the **cats**. Record her answer and the amount of time it took.

3. Cover the page again. Time her as she slides the paper from left to right and counts the **foxes**. Record her answer and the amount of time it took.

4. Finally, time her as she uses a pencil to cross out each **hippo** as she counts it. Record her answer and the amount of time it took.

5. Check the answer key (below) to see how accurate her counting was. Was she more accurate when using a paper to make lines or columns or when using a pencil to keep track?

6. Which did she count fastest: cows, cats, foxes, or hippos?

7. Which focusing method helped her the most? Did she do better moving her eyes across the page from left to right or did she do better scanning the page from top to bottom?

(Answer key: cows—12; cats—14; foxes—17; hippos—11)

Make Your Own Binoculars

A summer hike can be even more fun if children take binoculars with them. Let children have some fun making their own binoculars for close observations!

What you need: 2 toilet paper tubes, yarn, paper clips, hole punch or tape

What you do: Use the paper clips to fasten the toilet paper tubes together. Attach the yarn with tape or tie it through holes punched on each side of the binoculars so that they can be placed around the children's necks.

Magnets Attract _____ Box

Playing with magnets is fun and a great way to develop observational and focusing skills. You will need a large variety of small objects—paper clips, nails, buttons, bottle caps, wooden beads, brads, pencils, etc. Also provide a variety of large and small magnets. Invite children to experiment with attempting to pick things up with the magnets. Which objects will the magnets pick up? Arrange the paper clips on a piece of construction paper. Let children move the magnets under the paper. What happens? Put paper clips in a glass of water. Have children move the magnets around the outside of the glass. What happens? Give each child a magnet and invite the children to find things in the room that the magnets will attract. Put these objects in a box labeled "Magnets Attract _____."

Make Your Own Rainbows

Make a rainbow and see if children can observe all of its colors.

Rainbow 1: Go outside on a sunny day. Attach a nozzle to a garden hose so that it will make a fine mist or spray. To create a rainbow, make sure the sunlight is coming over your shoulder as you turn on the water. Invite children to share what they observed!

Rainbow 2: Use a prism to create a rainbow. A prism is a transparent glass object that is often shaped like a triangle. Hold the prism up in the sunlight. As the sunlight passes through the prism, the white light will separate into the colors of the rainbow. What colors do the children see?

∧∨∧

Make Your Own Kaleidoscope

Kaleidoscopes are terrific toys that provide opportunities for excellent observing experiences.

What you need: paper towel tube cut to 8" (20 cm) in length, clear plastic report cover, ruler, 4" (10 cm) square of black construction paper, 4" (10 cm) square of plastic wrap, 4" (10 cm) square of waxed paper, gift wrap or stickers, marker, scissors, rubber band, clear tape, colorful transparent beads, small sequins, shiny confetti

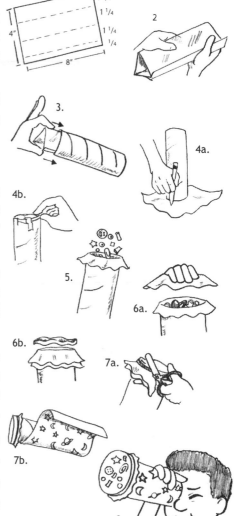

What you do:

1. Draw an 8" x 4" (20 cm x 10 cm) rectangle on the report cover and cut it out. Draw three lines 1¼" (3.1 cm) apart lengthwise across the rectangle as shown, leaving a ¼" (0.6 cm) edge along the bottom.

2. Fold the plastic along the lines to form a triangle-shaped tube. The ¼" edge overlaps on the outside. Use clear tape along that edge so that the tube stays closed.

3. Slide the plastic triangle tube into the paper towel tube.

4. Trace a circle around the end of the paper towel tube on the black construction paper and cut it out. Poke a hole through the center of the circle. Then, tape the circle over one end of the tube.

5. Place the square of plastic wrap on the other end of the tube. Press down gently to stretch the wrap and create a pouch inside the plastic triangle. Put beads, sequins, and confetti in the pouch.

6. Place the square of waxed paper over the pouch. Stretch the rubber band around the paper towel tube over both the waxed paper and the plastic wrap. Make sure the rubber band is tight enough to keep the beads, etc., inside.

7. Trim off the corners of the waxed paper and wrap. Decorate the outside of the paper towel tube with gift wrap or stickers.

8. Facing a light source like a lamp or window, hold the tube up to one eye and look through it. Slowly turn it to observe the colorful changing designs.

Scavenger Hunt

Invite the children in your class on a real scavenger hunt. Include objects on the list of things to find that will require them to use their observational skills. They might search for an object colored like your school colors or something that is hard, soft, made of wood, made of plastic, rough, smooth, tiny, big, long, or short. There are many descriptions that you can give the children. This fun activity encourages children to focus, concentrate, and observe closely as they search.

Dinosaur Bone Hunt

Cut out several kinds of dinosaur-bone shapes from heavy cardboard. Hide the "bones" outside or in the classroom. Invite children to pretend to be paleontologists, the scientists who study dinosaurs. Explain that paleontologists find dinosaur bones in the ground, and scientists have learned about dinosaurs by studying the bones. Have the children hunt to find the bones you have hidden. What did they learn by observing them?

Water Table and Sand Table Games

Water and sand tables provide children with excellent opportunities to observe and focus as they experiment to see if items sink or float and sift sand through funnels to fill containers of various sizes.

Paper Airplanes

Talk about airplanes. Compare pictures of some of the first airplanes to pictures of what planes look like today. Make paper airplanes to fly outdoors. Begin with a rectangular piece of paper. First, fold it in half lengthwise. Then, fold one corner down so that the short edge of the paper is on the lengthwise fold. Fold a third time so that the previous fold is on the lengthwise fold. Then, fold one more time. Flip the paper over and repeat with the other half of the paper. Take the airplanes outside for flying fun.

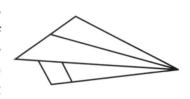

Air—We Can See What It Does!

It is not an easy task to explain to young children what air is. Say, "You cannot see air, but it is all around you—above you, behind you, and over you. Even though you cannot see air, you can see what air does and how it feels." Demonstrate with these objects to help children understand air.

Balloons: Say, "Air is what is inside a balloon when it is blown up. Air comes out when you let it go."
Soap Bubbles: Say, "Air is what is inside a soap bubble." Blow some bubbles with the children.
Straws and Bubbles: Blow through a straw into a glass of water. Say, "Air is what makes the bubbles."

Air—We Can Make It Move!

Cut standard 12" x 18" (30 cm x 46 cm) pieces of construction paper in half lengthwise; allow each child to decorate a piece and accordion fold it like a fan. (See illustration.) Children can use their fans to move air and see and feel its effects by fanning themselves, curtains, mobiles, etc. Use a fan to demonstrate that moving air is drying. Draw two squares of the same size on the blackboard. Wet both with a damp sponge. Fan one square and have children observe whether one square dries faster than the other.

Air and Rockets

If the weather is nice, go outside to allow room for children to run. Blow up a long balloon, release it, and watch it travel. Explain that this is how rockets push up into space. The children will want to chase the "rocket," so look forward to multiple launches and recoveries. (See the special note on page 2.)

Coordination and Concentration Games and Activities

Balloon Catch

What you need: inflated balloons (See the special note on page 2.), large funnels (If you do not have large funnels, roll pieces of tagboard into funnel shapes and tape them to tongue depressors for handles.)

What you do: Have a child place the balloon on the funnel and then push the funnel up to toss the balloon into the air. As the balloon comes down, the child should try to catch it on the funnel. This fun activity is very good for eye-hand coordination and muscle control. Children can play in groups and, as they become more adept, the group can count aloud each successful catch.

Party Games

Traditional birthday party games are easy to make, inexpensive, and fun. Let children take turns kneeling while facing backward on a chair, holding onto the chair back, and dropping items such as cotton balls, clothespins, or small plastic toys into containers such as coffee cans, boxes, or large plastic bowls.

Exercising on the Balance Beam

You will need a balance beam; this can simply be a 10' (3 m) plank that is 4" (10 cm) wide, or you can use masking tape to create the same size "beam" on the floor. Many children can participate if you tape lines on the floor to make several beams; if your children have no experience on a balance beam, be sure to try the exercises with tape first. When using a balance beam, always use a mat for safety.

Invite children to try the following:

1. Walk, toes pointed straight ahead, eyes looking down.
2. Walk, toes pointed straight ahead, eyes straight ahead.
3. Walk to the middle of the beam, turn, and walk back.
4. Walk backwards, arms extended to help with balance.
5. Hop in place on one foot.
6. Jump up and down on the beam, landing with one foot in front of the other each time.
7. Stand on one foot; swing the other foot back and forth.
8. Sit on the beam, feet straight out.
9. Sit on the beam with knees bent; then, straighten knees.
10. Walk with weight on all fours like an animal.
11. Bounce a ball while walking.
12. Throw a ball into the air and catch it while walking.

Toss-a-Shape Game

You will need 16 beanbags: four sets of four different geometric shapes (available commercially) or draw geometric shapes on regular beanbags. Divide a large sheet of paper (such as washable wallpaper) into four 8" (20 cm) squares. In each square, glue a different paper cutout geometric shape to match one of the four beanbag shapes. Cover the paper shapes with clear adhesive paper.

Four children can play this game. Each child chooses four beanbags with the same geometric shape and locates the matching shape on the paper. From a predetermined line, the children take turns tossing their beanbags, trying to get them in the squares with the matching shapes. The first child to land all of his beanbags in the matching square is the winner.

Ring Toss

Children love to play carnival games. Purchase or make your own ring toss game. Place four wooden dowels into an X-shaped piece of styrofoam as shown. Cut out the centers of plastic lids to create the rings. Set a kitchen timer for two minutes for each child to see how many rings she can land so that they encircle the dowels.

Bean Bag Fun

Place several containers in a straight row. Have a child stand behind a designated starting line and try to toss a beanbag into the first container. If successful, the child tosses the next beanbag into the next container and so on. Great containers (or boundaries) for tossing beanbags into include coffee cans, shoe boxes, hula hoops, and carpet squares.

Tower Building

Provide each child with the same number of building blocks. You can use traditional wooden blocks or clean, empty cans; milk cartons; boxes; etc. See who can build the highest tower before it falls. Children can also work together as a team, taking turns to add a block to their tower. Encourage children to look carefully at what they are doing and notice any signs that the tower is about to fall.

Name _____

Focus and Count

Improving Auditory Memory

Auditory Memory and Its Importance

The brain helps us remember in a variety of ways. First, the five senses gather information, which is then sent to the brain, stored, and retrieved (remembered) as needed. People can add memories to their brains by touching, seeing, tasting, smelling, and hearing. When information is added to the brain through the sense of hearing, it is called **auditory memory**.

Auditory memory is also the ability to recall the information we have heard and then stored in our brains. Developing auditory memory is an essential skill for everyday living. It allows people to accurately follow directions and helps them remember to accomplish daily tasks and perform various activities in the proper sequence.

Children who have a difficult time remembering things they have heard may have an auditory processing disorder (APD). Auditory processing disorders can occur in children without any other learning challenges, but many children with ADHD also have auditory memory difficulties. Since this is a challenge many children with ADHD encounter, it is imperative to provide them with activities that will increase their auditory memory skills.

There are many fun activities that can increase auditory memory skills. It is very important to choose games and activities that improve children's ability to focus. Memory skills—including the processes of listening, storing, and recalling information—can be significantly enhanced by simply improving a child's ability to focus.

As you prepare to introduce auditory memory activities, make sure that you reduce background noise and eliminate other distractions. Set the stage so that children will be able to focus to the best of their abilities.

Games and Activities to Improve Auditory Memory

What Did You Hear?

Choose a detailed passage from a story to read aloud. Tell children to listen very carefully because you will ask them to do something when you have finished reading. After reading, give each of the children a blank piece of paper and some crayons. Then, have children draw a picture and include as many details from the passage as they can recall. When children are finished drawing, read the passage again so that they can see how many things they remembered correctly. Let them add to their pictures the things they did not remember after the first reading of the passage.

Play Telephone

Playing the traditional game of telephone is actually an excellent activity for increasing auditory memory and for developing listening skills. Ask children to sit in a circle. Choose one child to whisper a sentence into the next child's ear. That child then whispers the same sentence to the next child and so on. Finally, when the sentence has gone the entire way around the circle, the last child says the sentence she heard out loud. More often than not, the sentence will have been altered in some way. The children will giggle with delight as they play this game, and they will become better listeners and develop stronger auditory memory skills.

Repeat after Me

Read a list of three or four words—only once—and then ask the children to repeat what they heard. As children improve in their ability to remember, increase the number or difficulty of the words. Children will also have fun working in pairs with one child reading a list of words and the other child repeating it. The first will have to listen carefully to discern if the other child is repeating the list correctly. As a challenge activity, ask children to repeat the lists backwards.

Variation: Complete the activity with sequences of numbers instead of words.

Rhythmic Clapping

Ask children to listen carefully as you clap your hands in a given pattern such as "short, short, long, short, long, long." Ask a child to clap back the identical sequence. Improvise using different patterns, as well as clapping loudly and softly. For a challenge, do not let the children see you clap—make them listen and then perform. Finally, let children take turns to lead the clapping.

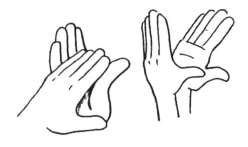

Variation: It is also fun to use a variety of rhythm instruments to create patterns for children to listen to and recreate.

Mnemonic Ideas

Mnemonic games are effective tools to help improve memory. We have all heard the mnemonic-device rhyme, "When two vowels go walking, the first one does the talking," to learn the sounds found in the vowel combinations of words like *boat*, *rain*, and *bean*. The phrase, "The principal is your pal," helps distinguish the difference in spelling between the words *principle* and *principal*.

Mnemonic spelling is a memory technique that has been useful for many children with reading disabilities. Choose a difficult spelling word and together come up with a silly phrase or rhyme. Here are some examples:

> **The**—**T**en **h**ens **e**at!
> **Said**—**S**he **a**lways **i**s **d**ancing.
> **Because**—**B**ugs **e**at **c**arrots **a**nd **u**se **s**ilverware **e**asily.
> **What**—**W**ild **h**orses **a**lways **t**rot.
> **Like**—**L**ook **i**n **K**arl's **e**ngine.
> **Was**—**W**ally **a**te **s**paghetti.
> **Here**—**H**arry's **e**agle **r**arely **e**ats.
> **There**—**T**he **h**uge **e**lephant **r**an **e**verywhere.
> **What**—**W**ho **h**as **a** **t**reat?

Grocery Store Shopping List

Tell children to pretend they are going to go to the grocery store. Say, "The refrigerator and cupboards are empty—we need lots of groceries!" Choose a child to name a grocery item such as bananas. The next child must say "bananas" and then add another grocery item like milk. The third child must say "bananas, milk" and then add a third grocery item and so on. How many items can your class remember for your grocery shopping trip?

To keep an accurate count, draw a grocery cart on the board and make a check mark for each word remembered.

Sequence the Day's Events

Variation 1: Ask a child to recall the events of the day or the events of the previous day. Challenge him to recall these events in the correct sequential order.

Variation 2: At the end of the day, ask children to recall sounds they heard during the day, such as an airplane, a dog barking, kids arguing in the hall, or a horn honking outside. Ask them when they heard each sound and write down the sounds in order. Count how many things they remembered hearing.

Singing

Singing is another fun way to encourage auditory memory. Many children who have had difficulty remembering math facts and spelling words have overcome these memory problems by putting the needed information to music. This is probably why many very young children are able to learn the alphabet so quickly. Most children are able to sing the ABC song even before they are able to recognize any written letters of the alphabet.

Following Oral Directions

Start this activity by telling the children that they are to listen very carefully and then do what has been asked. The object of the game is to see how many directions they can follow successfully. Begin with two directions such as "walk to the door and jump up and down." This will help the children feel some immediate success. Then, make the activity more challenging by increasing the number of directions so that children follow three directions, then four directions, and so on.

Variation: Find a magazine picture or use a page from a coloring book. Ask a child to follow a series of directions. For example, tell her to do three specific things to the picture, such as circle one thing, underline another, and put a square on the third. Have the child listen carefully to all three directions at once and then have the child perform the task on the paper.

Listen, Remember, and Follow the Directions Reproducible Activities (Pages 36–38)

The three reproducible activities on pages 36–38 will help increase auditory memory skills. Directions can be found on each individual activity page.

Name _____

Listen and Remember 1

Name _____

Listen and Remember 2

Directions for the teacher: The children will need a copy of this activity and crayons. Read these directions: **1.** Print your name on the line. **2.** Find the cave. Color it brown and draw a bear inside the cave. **3.** Find the doghouse. Color it green and draw a dog inside the doghouse. **4.** Find the pond. Color it blue and draw a duck swimming in the pond. **5.** Find the fishbowl. Draw a fish in the bowl and color the fish orange. **6.** Find the fence. Draw a pig by the fence and make the pig muddy. **7.** Find the cloud. Draw a bird above the cloud and color the bird blue.

Directions for the teacher: The children will need a copy of this activity and crayons. Read these directions: **1.** Print your name on the line. **2.** Find the bear. Color it brown and draw some berries by the bear. **3.** Find the fish. Color it green and draw some seaweed by the fish. **4.** Find the pig. Color it pink and draw a bow on the pig. **5.** Find the duck. Color it yellow and draw a piece of bread by the duck. **6.** Find the dog. Color it brown and draw a bone for the dog. **7.** Find the cat. Color it orange and draw a small mouse by the cat.

Where Do the Toys Belong?

Name _____

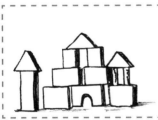

Directions for the teacher: Each child will need a copy of this page, crayons, scissors, and glue. Instruct the children to do the following: **1.** Print your name on the line. **2.** Now, everyone look at me and listen very carefully. I am going to read a story once. After listening to the story, you will cut out the toys and glue them where you heard the story say they should go in the child's room. **3. THE STORY: A little girl moved into a new house. She would like you to help her put her toys away. Listen carefully! She wants the bear on her bed. She wants the globe on the top bookshelf. She wants the blocks on the rug. And finally, draw the girl's face in the window.** (When the children have finished, read the story again so that they can check their work.)

The Tree

Name _____

✂ -

Directions for the teacher: Each child will need a copy of this page, crayons, scissors, and glue. Instruct the children to do the following: **1.** Print your name on the line. **2.** Now, everyone should look at me and listen very carefully. I am going to read a story once. After listening to the story, you will cut out the pictures of the animals and sun and glue them where they are supposed to go. **3. THE STORY:** Jack and Jill said, "What a beautiful day to go on a walk. I wonder what we are going to see on our walk. Oh look! There is a bird flying over the tree. And, look there! I see a squirrel under the tree. I hear something! It is an owl sitting up in the tree. What a beautiful day with the sun shining over us! (When the children have finished, read the story again so that they can check their work. For extra fun, ask children to draw Jack and Jill under the tree.)

Improving Visual Memory

Visual Memory and Its Importance

The introductory paragraphs in the preceding chapter, "Improving Auditory Memory," explained that people use their five senses to gather information. When information is added to the brain through the sense of sight, it is called **visual memory**. Visual memory is also the ability to recall the information that we have seen and then stored in our brains.

A great many children learn better by remembering what they have seen rather than by remembering what they have heard. But, for some children, remembering things that they have seen—such as the visual appearance of words or the order of letters in a word—can be a challenge. Visual memory skills can be enhanced with activities that help children learn to recall visual images of things they have seen.

Games and Activities to Improve Visual Memory

Picture This

Show the children a photograph. Let them study it for 20 to 30 seconds. Put the photo down and ask them to describe what they saw in the photograph.

Variation 1: After children have looked at the photograph, ask them questions about the photo, such as "What color was the car in the picture?" or "How many people were in the picture?"

Variation 2: If your students can read and write, have them look at the picture for a few moments and then cover it up. Using pencils and paper, ask them to try to write down every detail they can remember seeing in the picture. Then, have the children look at the picture again. Did they remember everything correctly? What details did they miss? Repeating this game with new photographs will help children build their visual memory skills.

What Do You See?

Place several small, familiar objects on a tray and cover them with a cloth or paper. Remove the cloth and expose the objects for a few seconds so that children can see them. Replace the cloth and ask a child to name as many objects as she can recall. Gradually increase the number of objects on the tray.

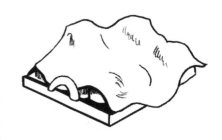

Variation 1: Place several objects under the cloth. Expose the objects for a few seconds. Ask the children to close their eyes; then, remove one object and rearrange the remaining objects under the cloth. Expose the objects again while the children try to recall which object is now missing.

Variation 2: Cover an illustration or photo depicting a number of items. Remove the cloth for a few seconds. Replace the cloth and have a child tell as much as he can about the objects he remembers seeing in the picture.

What Is Missing?

You will need a collection of five or six objects—these may be chosen by the children from available toys and materials in the room or may be flannel board felt cutouts—and a tabletop or tray.

Place the selected objects in full view for study. Then, choose one child to hide her eyes (or leave the room). Ask another child to remove one object. Have the first child uncover her eyes and guess what object is missing. If she succeeds, replace the missing object, and that child may decide what object to remove for the next round.

Variation: Instead of removing one object, change their arrangement or order. Then, the chosen child must replace the objects in their original order.

Arrange Us

Choose three or four children and place them in a line. (Increase the number of children in the line as their skills improve.) Have the rest of the class look at the line of children and then close their eyes. Rearrange the order of the children in the line. Ask the rest of the class to open their eyes and try to recreate the original line.

Variation: Place three or four objects in a row. Have the children look at the objects and then close their eyes while you rearrange them. Then, have the children open their eyes and try to place the objects back into their original sequence.

Concentration and Memory Matching Card Games

Memory match or other games like concentration are excellent for working on visual memory skills. Children can play with a standard deck of cards by making pairs of matching numbers and colors of suits. Use fewer cards—six to eight pairs of cards—with younger children.

1. Lay the cards facedown on a table in rows and columns.

2. The first player turns over two cards. If the cards match, the player keeps the pair and gets another turn. If the cards do not match, the cards are placed facedown again and play passes to the next player.

3. When all of the cards have been matched, the player with the most pairs wins.

Variations: For older children, use 39 cards (three of each kind); players turn over three cards for each turn to try to match all three. For an even greater challenge, use the whole deck and attempt to match all four cards in a suit. These versions can be quite difficult even for adults, so start easy and keep it fun.

Dominoes

Play a game of dominoes using large dominoes with either spots, shapes, or pictures on them.

 KE-804079 © Key Education —*"Pay Attention, Please!"*

Picture Puzzles

What you need: magazines, scissors, construction paper, glue sticks, watch or clock with a second hand, pencils, envelopes

What you do:

1. Give each player a magazine, scissors, a pencil, construction paper, a glue stick, and an envelope. Have each child cut out a picture from the magazine, cover the back with glue, and then carefully glue the picture on the piece of construction paper.

2. Invite the children to talk about their pictures with everyone in the class. Make sure that every child has seen every picture.

3. Next, have each child cut her picture into six puzzle pieces, writing her name on the back of each piece. Finally, each child should put her puzzle pieces in an envelope.

4. Collect the envelopes and then redistribute them—giving one to each child in the class. Alternatively, children may wish to trade puzzles with friends.

5. When you give the signal, the players take the puzzle pieces out of the envelopes, turn them over, and look at them carefully for one minute.

6. The players then have two minutes to assemble the puzzles.

7. After two minutes are up, see how many of the children were able to arrange the puzzle pieces correctly to see the original pictures.

What Is It?

Using real, everyday objects, hide one at a time behind a screen or another divider and slowly move the screen to reveal the object. Children may guess what the object is as soon as they recognize it. Try the activity again, using a bedsheet printed with simple, familiar picture outlines. The following will increase the difficulty of the activity:

◆ Use objects that children are not as familiar with.

◆ Use photographs.

◆ Increase the speed at which you reveal the objects or pictures.

◆ Use drawings that the children have created.

Movie Memory

Choose a several-minute segment from a DVD and show it to the children. Then, ask a series of prepared questions about what the children have seen. For example, "What color shirt was the boy wearing? How many animals were there? What was sitting on the table?" etc.

Look, Remember, and Follow the Directions Reproducible Activities (Pages 42–44)

The three reproducible activities on pages 42–44 will help increase visual memory skills. Directions can be found on each individual activity page.

Name _____

In the Garden

Picture 1

Picture 2

✂ -

Directions for the teacher: Each child will need a copy of this page and crayons or a pencil. First, show children how to fold this paper in half so that only one of the pictures can be seen. Then, tell children to look at **Picture 1**, allowing at least 10 to 15 seconds. The children should try to memorize each of the individual pictures. As they do this, they are viewing the pictures in isolation. When the time has elapsed, ask children to turn their papers over so that they can only see **Picture 2**. Ask them to find and color or circle the pictures they remember seeing in Picture 1. This task can be difficult because the children first must remember what they saw and then identify those pictures among other stimuli.

KE-804079 © Key Education —*"Pay Attention, Please!"*

Clowning Around

Name _____

Picture 1

Picture 2

Directions for the teacher: Each child will need a copy of this page and crayons or a pencil. First, show children how to fold this paper in half so that only one of the pictures can be seen. Then, tell children to look at **Picture 1**, allowing at least 10 to 15 seconds. The children should try to memorize each of the individual pictures. As they do this, they are viewing the pictures in isolation. When the time has elapsed, ask children to turn their papers over so that they can only see **Picture 2**. Ask them to find and color or circle the pictures they remember seeing in Picture 1. This task can be difficult because the children first must remember what they saw and then identify those pictures among other stimuli.

Ice Antics

Name _____

Picture 1

Picture 2

✂ -

Directions for the teacher: Each child will need a copy of this page and crayons or a pencil. First, show children how to fold this paper in half so that only one of the pictures can be seen. Then, tell children to look at **Picture 1**, allowing at least 10 to 15 seconds. The children should try to memorize each of the individual pictures. As they do this, they are viewing the pictures in isolation. When the time has elapsed, ask children to turn their papers over so that they can only see **Picture 2**. Ask them to find and color or circle the pictures they remember seeing in Picture 1. This task can be difficult because the children first must remember what they saw and then identify those pictures among other stimuli.

Helping Children Burn Energy

Why the Need to Burn Energy?

Children with ADHD sometimes have a great deal of excess energy. If the energy isn't used, they might display signs of hyperactivity such as fidgeting, squirming, running around, climbing, or talking excessively. The goal is to channel a child's excessive energy into acceptable activities.

A child with ADHD also has a special type of intensity, energy, and enthusiasm that can enhance life for her and those around her. Focusing on this energy as a positive quality, and having others do so as well, will greatly contribute to the child's self-esteem and academic success.

Building Awareness: Knowing When You Need to Burn Excess Energy

Discuss the concept of being aware of excess energy with the child. The more children know and understand about themselves, the better equipped they are to channel excess energy positively, instead of letting the energy cause problems. Here are some questions to help guide your conversation:

1. Do you think you have more energy than most children?
2. Do you think having a lot of energy is a good thing?
3. When you have to sit still but you feel like you want to jump around, what do you do?
4. Have you ever practiced sitting quietly for a few minutes?
5. Have you ever tried listening to soft, relaxing music to calm yourself?
6. Is exercise something you do every day?
7. Did you know that exercise is a good way to use extra energy?

Energy Burning Ideas

Help the child see that excess energy can be channeled and used for enjoyable purposes. Explain that he can release excess energy and get exercise while participating in many different sports and activities. Here are some suggestions:

◆ bicycling	◆ roller blading or ice skating
◆ yoga, kickboxing, or karate	◆ working out at a gym
◆ aerobics	◆ playing the drums
◆ jogging	◆ walking for a mile
◆ basketball, football, or soccer	◆ skiing or snowboarding
◆ running around a track	◆ camping
◆ jumping rope or skateboarding	◆ taking dance lessons
◆ playing follow the leader or tag	◆ hiking
◆ dog walking	◆ performing jumping jacks

Games and Activities to Burn Energy

Follow the Leader

Choose one child to be the leader and encourage the rest of the class to imitate the leader's actions. It is also fun to turn this "follow the leader" game into a "follow the animal" game. See how many different animals and their movements children can think of—bugs crawling, horses galloping, snakes slithering, bunnies hopping, worms wiggling, ducks waddling, etc.

Walking on Stilts

What you need: strong cord or rope, two large juice cans or small coffee cans.

What you do: Punch two holes on opposite sides on the bottom of each can.
Cut two pieces of cord that reach from the child's foot to waist and back. On each
can, poke the ends of the cord through the holes and tie them securely. The cords
should loop up to the child's hands for handles. Help the child up to practice
walking on the stilts while grasping a cord loop in each hand.

Jumping Rope

Jumping rope is a wonderful way to burn energy. Here are two counting rhymes children can chant
when they are jumping rope:

_____ likes to jump. _____ likes to count.   Going to the market, going to the store.
_____ knows her numbers. Listen as she counts.   We need some treats. How many more?

Hopping Races

Children love to hop and jump. Encourage this natural energy by providing children opportunities
to participate in a variety of hopping races, including the following:

- ◆ burlap sack races
- ◆ hopping backward races
- ◆ three-legged races (Preschoolers are not very good at this race, but they surely have fun trying!)
- ◆ hopping races on one foot
- ◆ races using big hops or little hops
- ◆ quiet, hopping on tip-toe races (End the races with this one.)

Free Dancing

Children love to dance, especially when they are allowed to move in any way they want. Provide
various accessories for children to use when free dancing to enhance the experience, for example:

- ◆ sheer scarves (Provide one per child.)
- ◆ balloons (See the special note on page 2.)
- ◆ jingle bells (Sew the bells on elastic bands to fit a child's wrist or ankle.)
- ◆ tom-toms or bongo drums
- ◆ flashlights (Cover the beams with colorful cellophane and use them to spotlight dancers.)

Zigzag and Other Ways to Run

This activity is very good for increasing spatial awareness. Make three long lines on the floor with
masking tape. The lines should be as far apart as your area will allow. Have children stand side by side
and spaced well apart on one of the outside lines. Then, have the children follow these directions:

- ◆ Run to the centerline, stop, and run back.
- ◆ Run in a zigzag fashion, crossing feet in front of each other, to the centerline and run back.
- ◆ Run to the farthest away line, stop, and run back.
- ◆ Run low to the ground to the centerline, alternating hands touching the floor, and run back.
- ◆ Run low to the ground to the farthest away line, touching the floor with both hands, and run back.
- ◆ Run sideways to the centerline, stop, turn a complete circle, and continue to the farthest
  away line. Repeat to run back.

Zoom!

Invite children to crouch down in an open space pretending to be rockets. Choose one child
to do the countdown. The child counts from 10 down to one and says, "Blast off! Zoom!" All of the
children can blast into space by leaping off their "launching pads." Have children fly around the room a
predetermined number of times and then return to their launching pads to prepare for another flight.

     KE-804079 © Key Education —*"Pay Attention, Please!"*

Improving Impulse Control

Impulse Control and the Challenges It Presents for Children with ADHD

A large percentage of children with ADHD have tremendous problems with impulse control. For these children, not being able to adequately control their impulsiveness can cause a multitude of difficulties; these are observed behaviorally and also seen in how the children react to situations without thinking, which sometimes results in making poor choices.

Children's lack of impulse control is evident in the following actions:

- They find it nearly impossible to wait in long lines, sometimes cutting into lines.
- They suffer, squirm, and complain as they wait for their turns.
- They often speak too loudly or will interrupt others.
- They frequently blurt out answers in class.
- Socially, they may say the wrong thing at the wrong time, being unaware that they have offended a classmate or hurt someone's feelings.
- And, sometimes, they may fight or argue with others because they have not taken the time—or were simply unaware of the need—to interpret a social situation correctly.

Children with these difficulties have narrow perceptions—they simply aren't able to "see the big picture" yet. These young children have not had enough experience to know that patience can be learned when it is practiced.

Ideas and Activities to Improve Impulse Control

Good Nutrition and Enough Rest

It is crucial for all children to eat well and get enough sleep to face the challenges of daily life. Children should always eat three well-balanced meals a day, as well as several healthy snacks. Regular bedtimes and calming bedtime rituals such as reading a book together or listening to soft music can help the restless child fall asleep more easily.

For children with ADHD, this is even more important. Children who are hungry or who have not had enough sleep will have even more trouble trying to curb impulses; they will probably be both more easily overstimulated and more frustrated. Sometimes the simplest solutions can solve the largest problems!

Stop and Think before You Speak

You can teach a child with ADHD to phrase things in a way that will get her point across without hurting someone's feelings. This may take some practice, but to make and maintain friendships, learning to be polite is a vital skill.

For a child with ADHD, telling the truth usually means blurting out the first thing that comes into her head. Without thoughts of malice, the child can unintentionally hurt others. Being prepared is the first step in learning appropriate communication skills. Use the questions on the following page to role-play and rehearse polite responses to situations which might inadvertently bring out the worst in her.

Sticky Situations:

1. A child in your class invites you to come and play at his house. If you don't want to go, how could you politely say no?

2. A girl in your class asks if you like her new dress. You do not think it is very special. How might you answer her in a polite way?

3. You are spending the night with a friend. The friend's mother serves liver and onions for dinner, which you hate. What could you do or say?

4. Your sister and her friends are watching TV. You don't like what they are watching. What will you do or say?

5. Your grandmother knits you a pea-green-and-orange striped sweater. It is fuzzy and too big, and you think it is ugly. She wants you to wear it to a party. What will you do and say?

6. Your baseball team is going out for pizza after the game. Since your team won, your mom wants to take you out for a hamburger to celebrate. You would rather be with the team. What might you say to your mother?

7. A boy says you took his pencil, even though you didn't. What will you say to him?

What! Consequences?

Children with ADHD are less likely to think before they act, and they usually act before considering the consequences—which can be disastrous. For these children, learning from their mistakes is often the best way to learn. When the child makes a mistake, take the time to discuss what happened and encourage him to verbalize what he learned from the experience.

Learning from mistakes can only happen when consequences occur. As a classroom activity, have the children find partners and then role-play each of the events listed below. After each pair is done performing, ask the children watching the performance these three questions: "What might be the consequences?" "What could be learned from the experience?" and "What would have been the better choice?" Discuss their responses.

Actions, Consequences, and Lessons Learned:

1. You stay up late watching TV instead of studying your spelling words.

2. You pack only candy in your lunch box.

3. A little kid is pushed in line and accidentally falls into you. Before you realize how small he is, you turn and shove him back.

4. Without asking permission, you borrow your father's saw to trim a tree.

5. You ignore your mom when she tells you to wear your coat to school. It rains that day.

6. You pretend to be sick so that you can stay home from school.

7. Your mom tells you to feed the dog before you go to school, but you forget.

8. You lose your house key and crawl inside through a tiny window when you get home.

9. Your teacher told the class there might be a pop quiz. You don't study because you think she was bluffing. She wasn't!

10. You tease your sister and make her cry.

KE-804079 © Key Education —"Pay Attention, Please!"

Rules and Consequences

Children with ADHD are often confused because they either do not understand the rules or do not understand the consequences of breaking the rules. Rules should be clearly understood by the child. Have a discussion about some of the rules in your classroom or at home:

- What is a rule?
- What are some of the rules you must obey?
- Can you name a rule you think is fair?
- Can you give me an example of a rule you think is unfair?
- Why are rules important?

List three basic rules that the children must follow. Use the reproducible chart below to record the consequences of breaking the rules and whether they believe the consequences are fair or unfair. Talk about the consequences they think are not fair. Together, talk about possible new—and more fair—consequences for breaking certain rules.

Rule: _____

Consequence: _____

Fair/Unfair: _____

New Consequence: _____

Rule: _____

Consequence: _____

Fair/Unfair: _____

New Consequence: _____

Rule: _____

Consequence: _____

Fair/Unfair: _____

New Consequence: _____

Prevent a Meltdown

Help children learn that there are ways to control impulses. As we have seen in the preceding activities, rehearsing responses, learning to stop and think before acting, and understanding the expected rules of behavior can be extremely helpful. It is also effective for children to use physical activity as a means of inhibiting some impulses. Children can be taught that when they are frustrated—an emotion that often leads to impulsive behavior—they can go for a walk, shoot baskets, or ride a bike, purposefully switching to an energy-burning activity that will help them compose and control themselves.

Overstimulated? Time to Relax

Children with ADHD sometimes turn little things into big things. A child overresponding to an event can escalate a problem that might have been solved by simply looking at the situation from another perspective. Learning to look at things in a variety of ways is a great skill to have, and children who can master this skill are happier.

Once a child goes "over the edge" or has a meltdown, there are things you can do to help the child recover. There are also techniques the child can be taught to help prevent these moments from happening in the first place.

Many children with ADHD benefit from scheduled periods of calm or quiet time. During these periods, playing relaxation games may be one of the best ways to help children relax and quiet down.

Create the Calm after the Storm

Return to Calm

Here are some quiet-time activities to bring a child back to a feeling of calmness:

Stories: Have children listen to a favorite story. Tell them to get comfortable in their chairs or on a rug. After the story, discuss how relaxed their arms and legs feel.

Music: Listening to music can have a comforting effect. Choose music that the children like and want to listen to. Celtic and classical music, as well as audio CDs of natural sounds like waterfalls and gentle rains, can be extremely soothing.

Deep Breathing: Teach children the following simple breathing exercise and when to use it to calm themselves. Demonstrate breathing deeply through your nose, holding your breath for a few seconds, and then exhaling air through your open mouth.

Exercise: Physical exercise is a great way to relieve tension. Jumping, hopping, skipping, and running can be very helpful to release and relax tight muscles. Talk about how the children feel after moving and loosening up their bodies.

Stretching: Stretching is another excellent way to release tension from muscles. Demonstrate some gentle stretches and invite children to follow along.

Relaxing Yoga

Traditionally, yoga has been used to develop body awareness while improving balance, muscular endurance, and strength. It can also be very relaxing. Use the Chart of Yoga Poses found on page 52 to help teach your students some of the basic poses that will stretch and build muscles. Many children delight in practicing yoga and enjoy learning the names of the poses they are doing.

Relaxation Games and Imagery Activities

The following series of ideas help children develop listening skills and encourage them to use their imaginations. You can try all of these ideas at once or you may wish to use them as separate activities. All have successfully provided quiet time and produced a calming effect on children.

Lying in the Sand

Invite children to stretch out on a rug or carpeted area. Say, "Imagine that you are at the beach. The sun is shining brightly. How does it make you feel? Your friend covers you with sand, letting it trickle over you slowly. How does it feel? Let the sand trickle over your body as I tiptoe once around the room."

KE-804079 © Key Education —"Pay Attention, Please!"

Strong as a Tree

Ask children to spread out in the room. Tell them to pretend they are trees, with branches reaching to the sky and their feet firmly planted on the ground for roots. Say, "Imagine feeling a breeze blowing gently through your branches. Slowly sway back and forth with the breeze. Now a storm is coming and the wind is getting stronger. How will you move? Remember you must stay planted in the ground. The wind is powerful as the storm is all around you. Now, the storm is passing and the wind is dying down. The breeze is gentle once again."

Palms for Pillows

Divide children into pairs. Have one child sit cross-legged with his hands together on his lap, open and palms up. The child's partner should lie faceup with his head resting on the first player's hands. Tell both players to close their eyes and remain quietly in these positions for about one minute. Then, ask partners to switch positions. Be sure to allow time for a follow-up discussion. How did each position feel? Was it easier to relax in one position or the other? Did their thoughts and feelings change when they switched positions?

Boat on the Water

Have children get on their hands and knees side by side on the floor. These children are the "ocean." Choose one child to be the "boat." This child lies down faceup across the ocean and closes her eyes. The children who are the ocean slowly sway to gently rock the boat. Tell the ocean that a storm is approaching. The boat must remain on the water as the waves become higher. Encourage the children who are the ocean to work together to keep the boat safe.

Flashlight, Flashlight

Gather together in the classroom or a gym and turn off the lights. Ask children to look straight ahead. Tell them to continue to focus forward while you shine a flashlight to the right side of them. Then, flash the light a certain number of times or move it in a particular pattern (making a circle, a square, etc.). Have children call out the number of times you flashed the light or name the pattern you made. Shine the light to the left side of the children to play again. This activity is good for visual memory and projection as well as peripheral awareness. It will also help develop the rapid eye movement necessary for reading.

Variation: A child can repeat the pattern with his own flashlight or children may work together to create and repeat each other's patterns. Children always think games and activities in the dark are fun!

Chart of Yoga Poses

(Directions can be found on page 50.)

Mountain—Tadasana

The Bridge—Setu Bandhasana

The Triangle—Trikonasana

Half Shoulder Stand—Ardha Sarvangasana

Dog and Cat

The Cobra—Bhujangasana

Sit Position—Sukhasana

Warrior II—Virabhadrasana II

Identifying and Understanding Emotions

An interesting quality that often accompanies ADHD is an intensity of feelings. Overresponding and being easily frustrated, excitable, and quick to anger are a few of the emotional traits and behaviors frequently seen in children with ADHD. Life becomes easier for these children when they learn how to take responsibility for understanding and managing their own ADHD—which includes learning how to identify, manage, express, and control their emotional states.

To assist children with learning in which areas they may need to become self-aware, copy and help them complete the questionnaire at the bottom of the page.

The Vocabulary of Emotions

To gain emotional strength, children must learn effective strategies for dealing with negative emotions such as sadness, disappointment, and embarrassment and with events that may be upsetting. Managing and not overresponding to positive emotions is equally as important. In order to develop these skills, children must learn the correct vocabulary and be able to identify emotions in themselves and in others. The ability to name a feeling is the first step towards being able to manage it. It is also important that children realize that all emotions are OK. There is no such thing as a good or bad feeling—there are just good and bad ways of handling the feeling.

Make two copies for each child of the faces on page 57. First, talk about each picture's facial expression. What do children think the child is feeling? Why? Then, let the children color both pages of faces, cut them out, and use them to play memory match.

- -

Self-Awareness Questionnaire

1. Do you dislike making changes? _____

2. Is it hard for you to pay attention? _____

3. Do you have difficulty planning ahead? _____

4. Do you often feel restless? _____

5. Do you hurt people's feelings by talking without thinking first? _____

6. Are you sometimes reckless, and do you do dangerous things? _____

7. Do people say you fidget (drum fingers, swing legs, tap feet, etc.)? _____

8. Do you make snap decisions that don't work out? _____

9. Do you overreact to pressure? _____

10. Do you get angry easily? _____

11. How do you show your anger? _____

12. Do you make big deals out of unimportant things? _____

13. Do people say you are moody? _____

Cut and Paste a Face Reproducible Activity (Page 58)

Copy Cut and Paste a Face on page 58 for each child. Have children color, cut out the facial features, and then play with arranging them on the blank face. Have them name each facial expression they create with the different features. When they are finished experimenting with all of the features, let each child choose a favorite arrangement and glue it in place.

Understanding the Feeling of Anger

Understanding Our "Sometimes" Anger

Many children with ADHD overreact when they are under pressure. One extreme response to various stressors is to strike out at others. It is paramount that children with ADHD learn how to handle conflict without resorting to fighting. (Parents often comment that their children with ADHD tend to overreact in negative ways, but, on the positive side, they also enjoy their children's enthusiasm when the overreaction is one full of joy and excitement.)

Guide children to understand that anger isn't a bad thing; it is a signal that something is wrong. Let children know that all people get angry—it's how we react to the feeling of anger that can get us into trouble and make us feel powerless. Explain that you will help children learn how to deal with anger in socially acceptable ways. Use the following questions to talk about anger and discuss some appropriate responses, such as working out a compromise, walking away from a tense situation, talking with an adult about the problem, etc.

1. Do you sometimes overreact?
2. What makes you the angriest?
3. What do you do when you get angry?

Making Anger Go Away

To help a child with ADHD deal with anger—or its underlying causes such as feeling hurt, unfairness, fear, frustration, helplessness, or guilt—in socially acceptable ways, talk with the child about his experiences with strong, and sometimes heated, emotions.

1. Do you know the differences between feeling hurt, being treated unfairly, being afraid, or feeling frustrated?
2. Tell about a time when you felt cheated.
3. What is the scariest thing you can think of?
4. What is the most frustrating experience that you can recall?
5. Can you describe a time when you felt hurt?

Assisting the child in identifying underlying feelings behind anger will make it possible for her to deal with her feelings appropriately. Say, "Some children believe that being angry is a bad thing. It isn't wrong to feel angry; all people get angry sometimes." Ask, "Would you like to learn some ways to make your anger (hurt, feelings of unfairness, fear, or frustration) easier to deal with?"

A beneficial strategy when dealing with anger is to experiment with calming and relaxing techniques. These can be found in the chapter "Overstimulated? Time to Relax" on pages 50–52. Many of these ideas will be helpful in reducing feelings of anger.

Good and Bad Ways to Get Angry Reproducible Activity (Page 59)

Copy Good and Bad Ways to Get Angry on page 59 for each child. This activity will prompt discussion and help children identify appropriate ways to show anger. Complete directions can be found on the reproducible page.

 KE-804079 © Key Education —"Pay Attention, Please!"

Understanding the Feeling of Sadness

Talk about How You Feel

One of the most simple and effective means of coping with sadness is for cildren to talk about their feelings of unhappiness. Help children identify people whom they trust and would feel comfortable talking to. Remind children that sadness is OK, and that everyone feels sad from time to time.

Creative Outlets

Children have the natural ability to use play and creativity as outlets that can help them process and begin to understand their emotions. Provide children with opportunities to express themselves and their feelings through drawing, writing, painting, sculpting, dancing, and simply playing. Encourage children to talk about what they have created.

Exercise

Exercise is a natural antidepressant. It produces endorphins and promotes general physical and mental well-being. Use the games and activities found in the chapter "Helping Children Burn Energy" on page 45 to assist with elevating a child's mood.

If You Had One Wish . . . What Would It Be? Reproducible Activity (Page 60)

Copy If You Had One Wish . . . What Would It Be? on page 60 for each child. Have children draw pictures of their wishes and then share them with the class.

Understanding the Feelings of Fear and Anxiety

The Broad Spectrum of Fear and Anxiety

Fear and anxiety cover a broad spectrum, including normal, everyday fear such as the fear of being rejected, looking silly, being embarrassed, or getting physically hurt. There are also exaggerated fears or phobias. Some common childhood phobias include being afraid of the dark, certain animals, heights, or storms.

Embarrassing Moments Reproducible Activity (Page 60)

Copy Embarrassing Moments! on page 60 for each child. Discuss the events shown and encourage children to share similar experiences if they feel comfortable doing so. Emphasize that everyone has faced an embarrassing moment at one time or another.

When Something Scares You . . . What Should You Do? (Page 61)

Copy When Something Scares You . . . What Should You Do? on page 61 for each child. Each of the four illustrations depicts a child sharing concerns with a caring adult. Complete directions can be found on the reproducible page.

Happiness and Friendship

Start the School Year with Smiles and Friendship

How exciting to begin school! So many new faces! Children are generally excited about their first day of school, but they are also a little apprehensive about all of the people they have yet to meet. Spend some time talking about the new friendships they will make this year. Introduce each of the children to the class. More verbal children may wish to introduce themselves. Take a photograph of each child first thing in the morning. If possible, print them right away, label them with names, and then pass the photos around for all of the children to see. Let children take turns saying their names into a tape recorder and then play back the recording for the whole class to hear.

Great Rules for Making and Keeping Friends

◆ **Excellent Etiquette**

Discuss with children the term *manners*. Good manners are more than being polite; they are also ways that children can show respect and consideration for others.

◆ **Magic Words**

Please and *thank you* are the traditional "magic words." Talk about the fact that these are words people enjoy hearing. When asking for something or when someone has done something nice, it is always right to say "please" and "thank you."

◆ **Being a Good Listener**

Tell children that when their parents, a teacher, or any other person is talking, it is respectful and considerate to be a good listener. Ask, "How do you feel when you are trying to talk and the person to whom you are talking is not listening?"

◆ **Greeting People**

People like to be looked in the eyes when they are talking. Say, "Do you like to talk to people who are looking at the ground and not at you? When you greet someone or meet someone new, look at him when you say 'hello' with a big smile." Talk about how warm and friendly faces help people to feel welcomed.

◆ **Sharing**

Sharing is not always an easy task—especially when you are young! Discuss with children why it is important to share. Emphasize that sharing is also a good way to make and to keep friends.

◆ **I'm Sorry**

We have all said things on occasion for which we are sorry. Tell children that everyone makes mistakes. Point out that if a child has made a mistake or has hurt someone's feelings, it is good to say, "I'm sorry" as soon as possible.

◆ **Be Fair**

Everyone wants to be treated fairly. Have children list ways to show fairness, such as not breaking in line, pushing ahead of others, or bossing their friends.

◆ **Respect and Consideration**

Ask children if they know what "being considerate" means. Talk about how it is important to respect another person's feelings; then, share examples of situations where someone was considerate. If everyone could remember the two words *respect* and *consideration*, the world would be a much more congenial place to live!

Happy

Sad

Sleepy

Afraid

Excited

Hungry

Silly

Angry

Nervous

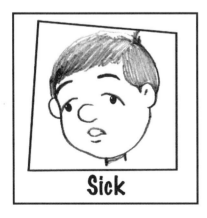

Sick

Bored

Wild Card

Cut and Paste a Face

Directions for the teacher: Have children cut and paste the features to make a happy, a sad, or an angry face.

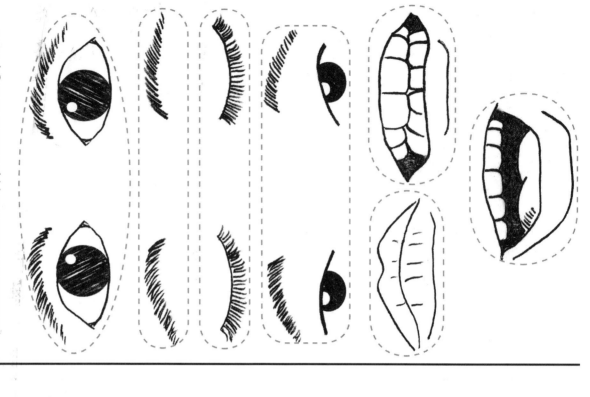

Name _____

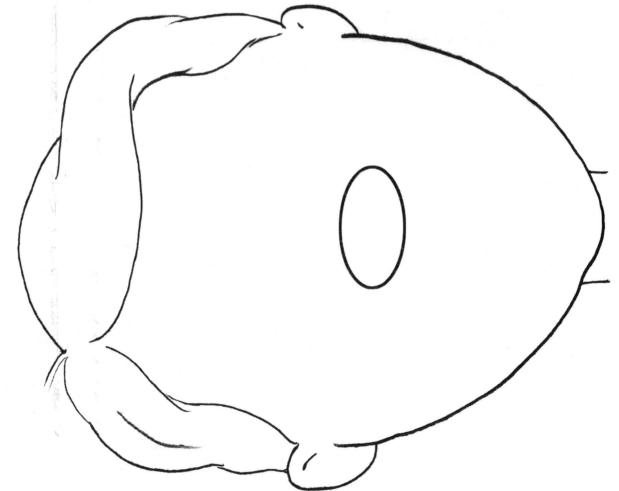

Name _____

Good and Bad Ways to Get Angry

Directions for the teacher: Discuss with the children how it feels to be angry. Have children circle the pictures that show appropriate ways to show anger. Put an X on the inappropriate ways to show anger.

1.

2.

3.

4.

5.

6.

Name _____

Embarrassing Moments!

Directions for the teacher: Discuss the events below. These things happen to everyone!

Name _____

If You Had One Wish.... What Would It Be?

KE-804079 © Key Education —"Pay Attention, Please!"

Name _____

When Something Scares You—What Should You Do?

Directions for the teacher: Discuss each of the illustrations with the children.
Encourage them to take this page home and share it with their parents.

1.

Talk to a teacher.

2.

Talk to a parent.

3.

Talk to a grandparent.

4.

Talk to a trusted adult.

Building Self-Esteem

Self-Esteem and Its Importance

Children with ADHD hear more than their share of criticism, which can cause serious harm to their self-esteems. We know that children who feel good about themselves are willing to try harder. They are not as fearful of failure and are willing to admit mistakes and take chances. Children with ADHD are often confronted with challenging situations. They must develop strong senses of self-esteem, which will help them better control impulsiveness, focus their attention, and become responsible problem solvers. Children with ADHD are typically some of the most energetic, enthusiastic, alert, creative, and perceptive students.

Offer Praise and Immediate Feedback

All children thrive on positive reinforcement and love being told that they have done a good job. But, children with ADHD need feedback and praise that is immediate as well as genuine. When a child with ADHD doesn't get the acknowledgement that he needs, he usually will not know how to ask for it. Remember to praise not only the successes, but also all good efforts. Children will keep trying and continue to learn if they are praised for effort as well as for progress.

Games and Activities to Build Self-Esteem

What's Good about Me?

Discuss with the children the idea of building character—all those attributes that help us become who we want to be. To find out what characteristics children think they would like to develop, play the following game.

Directions: On individual index cards, have children write down the descriptive words listed below; you may add additional descriptive words. Read and explain the words on the cards to the children. Help them sort the cards into three piles: character assets, traits they want to develop, and traits they do not feel are important.

adventurous	attentive	calm	cooperative	curious
empathetic	empowered	enjoys learning	expressive	flexible
forgiving	friendly	generous	gentle	good listener
grateful	healthy	honest	humorous	imaginative
inquisitive	kind	learns from mistakes	loving	patient
polite	problem solver	reliable	responsible	self-motivated
truthful	will ask for help			

After sorting the cards, have children make a poster about themselves. Encourage them to use descriptive words from the index cards.

Daily Journaling

Some characteristics typical to ADHD children are extremely positive, but if children do not recognize their strong points, they cannot celebrate them. Help children discover which positive ADHD characteristics are part of their personalities by responding to the journal starters on the next page.

Positive characteristics journal starters:

- ◆ Are you artistic? What do you like to create?
- ◆ Are you friendly? Do you enjoy meeting new people?
- ◆ What is your favorite thing to do?
- ◆ If someone asked you if you have a special talent, what would you say?
- ◆ What do you like best about yourself? What do you think people like best about you?
- ◆ What would you like to be when you grow up? Why?

Autobiography

Ask parents to send to school four or five photographs of their child through several stages of growth, beginning with a baby picture and perhaps one for each year thereafter. Make an autobiography booklet for each child. Fold a 9" x 12" (23 cm x 30 cm) sheet of colored construction paper in half for the cover. Copy the photographs on a color copier, centering two pictures on each 8.5" x 11" (22 cm x 28 cm) paper. Then, cut these pages in half so that there is one image per page. Have the child dictate or write a story about the circumstances of each photograph and add the story under each picture. Place the pages in chronological order and staple them between the construction paper covers. (Be sure to send the photographs home as soon as you are done duplicating them.)

(Directions: Copy, cut out, and use often to boost self-esteem.)

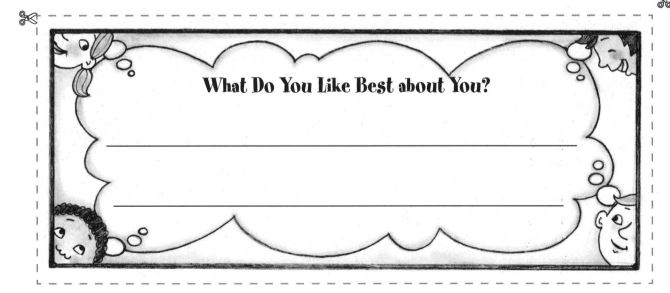

Notes